BLUEPRINT
to
BEHAVIOR

ADAPTING TO AUTISM IN YOUR FAMILY BY
UNDERSTANDING BEHAVIORS.

Meghan Ashley, MSCP, LPC-S

ISBN: 979-8-9866490-0-9

Printed in United States

Published by Meghan Ashley via Amazon and Ingram Spark

Foreword

I am honored to write the foreword for this remarkable book, "Blueprint to Behavior" by Meghan Ashley. As someone who has had the privilege of knowing Meghan personally and professionally, I can attest to her extraordinary dedication, insight, and compassion for the autistic community.

My relationship with Meghan began when our paths crossed due to my conference. Meghan submitted a proposal to be a speaker. From the moment I heard her speak while interviewing her for my podcast, I was captivated by her deep understanding of the challenges faced by autistic individuals and their families. Her ability to articulate the complexities of autism with clarity and empathy was truly inspiring.

One of the most profound impacts Meghan has had on my life was through her guidance in understanding the unique behaviors associated with my own late diagnosis as a Black autistic individual. Navigating a world that often misunderstands and overlooks our experiences can lead to moments of deep confusion and frustration. Meghan's insights and practical advice have been a beacon of hope during these times. She has an exceptional ability to translate complex psychological concepts into relatable, actionable steps that individuals can take to better understand and support themselves, particularly within our community. Her approach is rooted in empathy and respect for the individual, emphasizing that behavior is a form of communication and a powerful expression of our identity.

Meghan's work has helped countless families like mine. Through her counseling practice, workshops, and now this book, she has provided invaluable support to autistic individuals, parents, caregivers, and educators striving to understand and care for autistic children or themselves. She has an uncanny ability to see the world through the eyes of her clients, offering them tailored strategies that address their specific needs and circumstances. Her practical, compassionate approach has empowered many to move from a place of frustration to one of understanding and proactive support.

One of the most compelling reasons Meghan is uniquely qualified to write this book is her extensive professional background and personal experience. Meghan holds a Bachelor of Arts in English and Psychology from LSU-Baton Rouge and a Master of Science in Counseling Psychology from LSU-Shreveport. Her academic achievements are impressive, but what truly sets her apart is her hands-on experience. Meghan is autistic herself and is raising autistic children, which gives her a profound and personal understanding of the journey. She has worked in various settings, including higher education, inpatient and outpatient therapy, and as a behavior specialist. This rich tapestry of professional and personal experiences informs her holistic and empathetic approach to autism and behavior change, making her insights especially valuable and authentic.

In this book, Meghan delves into the intricacies of behavior among autistic children, offering readers a comprehensive guide to understanding and supporting them. She explores the reasons behind various behaviors, providing a nuanced perspective that goes beyond surface-level observations. Meghan emphasizes that behaviors are not random or purposeless; they are often a response to unmet needs, sensory experiences, or communication challenges. By understanding these underlying factors, parents and caregivers can develop more effective and compassionate strategies for support.

One of the strengths of Meghan's approach is her focus on individualized care. She recognizes that every autistic child is unique, with their own set of strengths, challenges, and preferences. Her strategies are not one-size-fits-all but are tailored to meet the specific needs of each child. This personalized approach is a testament to Meghan's deep respect for the individuality of each person she works with.

I am confident that this book will have a profound impact on its readers, just as Meghan has had on the countless individuals and families she has worked with. Her compassionate approach and unwavering commitment to improving the lives of autistic individuals make her a true advocate and ally. It is with great admiration and respect that I recommend this book to you.

Sincerely,

Maria Davis-Pierre, LMHC

Autism in Black® CEO

CONTENTS

Chapter 1

INTRO TO THE BLUEPRINT TO BEHAVIOR

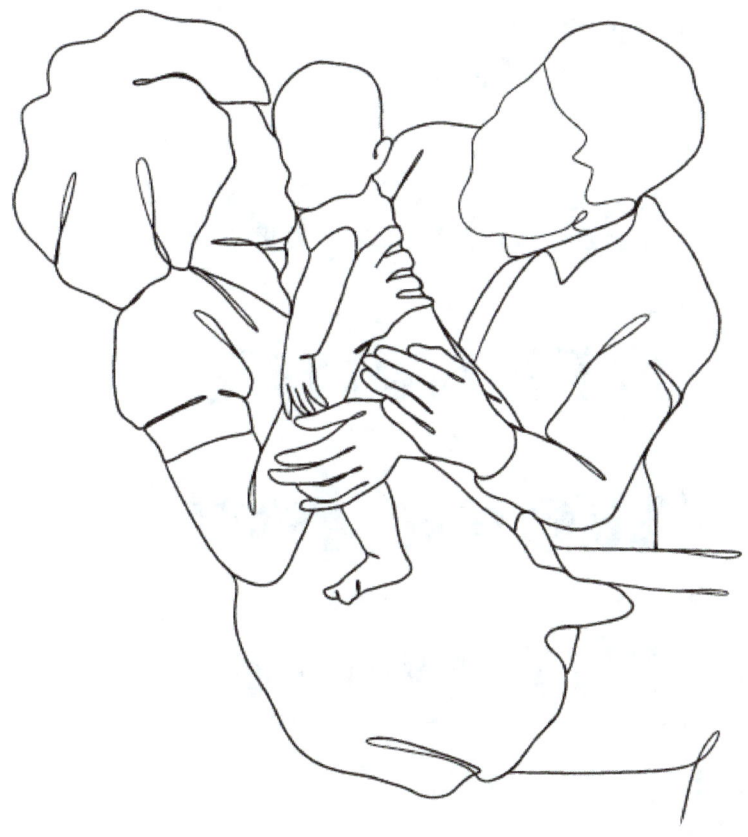

"The basics of behavior work for everyone"

Meet The Author

Hey, Ya'll!

I'm Meghan Ashley. If you know me, you know I wear a lot of hats in my life. At any given time, I am a:

- Licensed Professional Counselor

- Former Educator

- Business Owner

- Author

- Autism Specialist

- Most importantly, Mom to two amazing Autistic kids

So what qualifies me to teach you how to help your family with the behaviors that come with Autism? All of it! The combined experience I have in the trenches with my own kids and the knowledge base from my profession meet beautifully in this book. Everything I recommend, I've tried already. Everything I've tried hasn't always worked, and I have learned just as much from my failures as from my successes.

Chances are, you've had some "parenting failures" on the Autism journey too because there is no right way to do this. Every family, Autistic person, and life experience is different.

I've packaged everything I've learned about behavior into this book so you don't have to reinvent anything. Just work through the book. You are not alone out here in these parenting streets!

The goal is to give you a blueprint from where you are to where you want to go, and to have you fill in the particular details along the way. This book is meant to be experienced, not just read through. There will be things for you to fill out, try with your child, and revisit. You will try, fail, cry, track, try again, succeed, track, cry, rinse, wash, repeat.

In the end, you will leave with an individualized plan for your child and your family that leads to more good days than bad, and helps you adapt to the autism that is a part of your life. I am ecstatic you are here. The thought of another family living their best Autistic lives just brings me joy. 👣

Let's dig in and get started!

Meghan Ashley

FREQUENTLY ASKED QUESTIONS

If we have speech therapy, occupational therapy, ABA therapy and any therapy that has been invented, why do I need this book?

This book does not replace the one-on-one therapies your child receives. It is written specifically for the caregivers of autistic children so that they can feel more comfortable with autism. The therapists working with your child may provide tips on how to transfer the skills learned in therapy to your everyday life, but most of what they do is effective when your child is with them. The information here bridges the gap.

Once I learn the information for the age my child is now, will I need to learn it again for their next phase of development?

No. The information here is the building blocks of all behavior across the lifespan. Once you learn the basics it can be applied forever.

Should my child's other parent or other caregivers read this book too?

Sure they can! The more informed people in your child's life, the better. I advise that if others don't read this book, you relay the information learned to them so that all caregivers for your child are working together.

Will the information learned work for my other Neurotypical children also?

Yes. The basics of behavior work for everyone. The Autism specific information is listed as such.

How long will it take to complete this book?

That is up to you. The book is self-paced but you do have to complete one section before you will have enough knowledge to move to the next since each section's information builds on the previous one.

If I get confused and need help, what can I do?

Reading and going at it with just the book may not be for you. I have different individual coaching plans that may better suit you that come with my time and guided instruction at M.perfectconsulting.com.

TOOLS YOU WILL NEED

- Gather a notebook or binder exclusively for this book. You don't want to be searching for a receipt where you wrote that nugget of information.
- Print the pages provided for writing information. Worksheets are in the back of the book and can be purchased digitally at adaptingtoautism.com.
- Have something to write with: a pen, pencil, or marker—whichever you prefer.
- You will need access to your child to conduct research and test the interventions you learn. Winging it with assumptions will not work.
- Extend grace to yourself. This is a process and it may take a while. Remember this when you feel frustrated.

Chapter 2

THE RESEARCH-OBSERVING AND ASSESSING

"The magic word for making everywhere Autism friendly is ACCOMMODAT IONS"

The Magic Word Is...
Accommodation

In this section you will learn:

- What they need, what their behavior is trying to tell you, and what they don't want or need.
- Where they need accommodations to help them out.
- When it is time for you to step in and help them help themselves.
- How to get all of this information.

The Magic Word Is....

Alright, so here we are in the thick of things.

Your child has a diagnosis, you are getting the services your child needs, and you are waiting for everything they are learning to kick in and all of your Autism related challenges will disappear, right? Yeah, nope. It doesn't work like that!

We are adapting to Autism, not temporarily accepting it in hopes that it will change soon. The best way to adapt is by changing the behaviors of everyone in your child's environment and reducing factors that can cause a meltdown. In this program you can still tell your child "no," let them be disappointed, and not give in to all their wishes.

My unpopular opinion is that behavior management is the responsibility of the adults around the child. They must create an environment where the child can achieve the highest possible level of success. It's not your child's job to "behave" in situations where they cannot manage their own behaviors. It just doesn't make sense.

Make every place your child goes a place where they can feel comfortable and in control of their impulses and emotions. Sounds like a magical world that doesn't exist, right?

Before you trash this book and give me negative reviews on google, hear me out. I will show you how to make this happen for your child.

The magic word for making everywhere Autism friendly is **ACCOMMODATIONS.**

Simple Assessing For Accommodations

Accommodations need to be appropriate to the situation and helpful to your child. Period.

Noise-canceling headphones don't fix everything. You will need more than that. In the next few steps, you will learn how to craft creative accommodations for your child's care team.

Ask your child by verbalizing questions to them or observing their behavior. What are their triggers and soothers? Use the "Assessing for Accommodations (A-4 to A4e)" sheet to ask specific questions.

Example questions are:

- What makes you feel yucky?
- What does yucky feel like?
- Who makes you feel safe?
- Where do you feel safe?
- When do you normally feel like running away?
- What does your body do when you know you are ready to leave a place?
- Who makes you feel better?
- What helps you calm yourself?

- Where do you love going/ hate going?
- Create your own questions based on your child and their behaviors.
- Use your own observations and ask yourself these questions about the last time you were out with your child and a meltdown occurred.

The questions should start with who, what, where, or when. Notice I don't ask why. Most people, autistic or not, don't know the precise reason why they took that action and why questions tend to increase frustration all around. You could ask them why if you want, but I wouldn't make it the main way to understand what they need as they may not understand why they need what they need. We will work on the "why" in later lectures.

Write the answers to these questions on a blank sheet of paper and use the information to fill in the worksheet with the different places your kid goes and what they need in each place. Create the accommodations based on this info in the If_____, then_____ format.

For example, If we are in the car and my child is squirming and squinting, then I will pull down their sunshade.

The question you ask yourself is: what are their observable behaviors?

Answer: they are showing fidgety behaviors and they fidget when uncomfortable.

Second question: what is making them uncomfortable right now?

Answer: the sun is in their eyes.

Last question: What can I do to lessen that discomfort.?

Answer: when they had the same behavior yesterday, they couldn't reach the sunshade and needed help that they didn't know how to ask for which caused a meltdown.

Today, I will lower the shade for them well before they are in enough discomfort to cry out. Resolution: they immediately show signs of comfort again, smiling and swinging their feet after the shade blocks out the pesky sun.

Ready for another example?

Okay!

If we go to the grocery store and my child puts their hands over their ears, then I will offer them their earplugs for noise comfort. We are in the grocery store. My child is walking next to me, and I keep asking them to keep their hands on the basket, but they keep putting them up to their ears. I don't hear anything out of the ordinary, but my child looks pained and looks up at the lights.

Question: What is making them cover their ears?

Answer: The music in here is a little loud, and they have complained that the fluorescent lights buzz and hurt sometimes, too. I don't know the exact trigger, but I know that it is noise that is bothering them.

Question: what can I do to help lessen their discomfort?

Answer: Hand them their noise-canceling earplugs that block out background noises but still allow them to hear me when I talk to keep them safe.

Resolution: I hand them the earplugs. They quickly put them in, and the look of relief on their face and the hug they gave me in aisle 5 brought me to tears. We can now continue shopping.

Accommodations In Action

Accommodations in action usually involve compound accommodations, or you are using more than one accommodation per scenario to ensure your child gets what they need. In the scenarios below, the children require multiple questions to be asked and accommodations made in order for them to be helped. Test your knowledge by reading the description, stopping to assess what accommodations you would use, and then read what I wrote afterwards.

JIMMY

Jimmy howls all summer when he has to get in the car. Mom notices that he resists getting buckled in, screams until they get home, and bolts out of the car as soon as possible. Jimmy fidgets in his seat and holds his legs up in an uncomfortable position for every ride. When they get home, he is sweaty and inconsolable. Jimmy sits in the backseat in a front-facing booster seat, as he is 7 years old.

What could be the reason for Jimmy's behavior?

A. He hates the car and nothing will help this. He will hate the car forever and we all will suffer for it.

B. Jimmy is showing discomfort. Let's investigate possible reasons.

B is right; his behavior is signaling a fixable issue. Let's check out all five of Jimmy's senses to determine some possible accommodations to be made.

Touch: It's hot out here y'all, and these leather seats are sizzling. You can put a blanket over Jimmy's booster so the buckles don't get hot in the sun during the day. You can put a blanket under his legs when he sits so that his skin never touches the leather. You can have ice packs in the car for him daily.

Taste: No indication of an issue here, but having a calming snack can help.

Smell: No indication of an issue here, but calming scents can help.

Hearing: Even though there is no indication of an issue here, noise-canceling headphones can help with the potentially overwhelming buzzing and popping sounds of being in a car.

Sight: If it's hot, then it's probably also bright. Let Jimmy pick out some cool sunglasses or put up a sun shade for his window if he prefers.

Bonus accommodations: If you are hot, he probably is too, so having a cool drink and a personal fan can save some anguish. They even have air conditioning extenders or backseat fans that can help air reach the back of your car and your kids better.

Accommodations are in place and now we have a happy kid. He is feeling cool, calm, regulated, and cared for. Where he used to dread the car, now he can ride in peace due to his personal accommodations. Good job parent!!

ANNA

Anna is a 5-year-old autistic who is semi-verbal and lives for the park. The swings are her favorite, and she could stay on them all day. Her father would like to go home, so he goes to round up Anna and her 7-year-old neurotypical sister, Kate. He yells across the park, "Girls, it's time to go now!" Kate hops off the monkey bars and comes running to her dad. Anna is still swinging as if she didn't hear her father. Dad walks up a bit and yells again. Anna doesn't stop. Dad goes up to the swing, stops it, and picks up Anna while scolding her. Anna starts screaming, makes herself limp, and falls to the ground. Anna becomes more and more agitated and shrill the more her father yells and tries to control the situation by repeating his request. Dad gets fed up, picks up Anna kicking and screaming, and shoves her into her car seat and drives off. Anna is inconsolable, and Dad is frustrated and embarrassed with the situation.

Should Dad have;

A. Expected Anna to obey his first command.

B. Use her accommodations to help her navigate the disappointment of leaving a highly preferred activity.

B is right again!

Dad could have handled Anna gently and mindfully. First, he could have gotten her off the swings after she had been on them for a while and gently coaxed her to play with a lower preferred item like the slide. The transition from the slide to the car is less jarring. Then he could wait until Anna came down the slide, get eye level with her, and tell her where they are going next, like "Anna, it's time to go home and eat pizza. Hop on my back; let's go!" It can help if he shows her a picture of the pizza, and then a picture of their car. He can also have a small sweet or a small favorite rarely seen toy to help her transition to the car. He can say, "Do you want this sweet or this toy right now?" and give her what she chooses. None of the options he gives her include the swing. If she tries to go back to the swings, Dad could pick her up before she gets there or hold her hand while she walks with him so she can't return, then get at eye level with her and tell her, "Anna, it's time to go," and then lead her to the car.

Dad can also "swing" Anna in his arms to give her a similar sensory input that she gets from the stationary swings as he is guiding her to the car. Dad can then tell Kate it's time to go, and Anna can follow with Kate while they hold hands on the way to the car.

Dad is not to let Anna return to the swings because it would lead to a power struggle when she has to leave. Also, Dad doesn't need to say, "I know you are sad to leave the swings," because the focus is not on leaving; it is on going to the next thing. Notice in the accommodated example, that Dad never yells, always focuses on Anna's needs, and keeps giving her attention and care. Even if Anna has a meltdown, she knows her father is a safe space and that he will not escalate the situation by losing his cool also.

Dad can praise Anna for coming back to the car so well and make sure that he keeps the promise of pizza to continue to build trust between them. If Anna is upset while going to the car, Dad can get her there and buckled in before he tries to calm her and validate her feelings. The number one concern is her safety, and you don't want her to be in a position where she can run back to the swings and potentially put herself in harm's way in a parking lot.

Dad can then attend to all five of her sensory needs and ensure she is comfortable and safe before driving off. Using all of her accommodations does not guarantee that she won't be upset when leaving the park; it just gives her a calmer leaving the park experience so that she can go more often.

No parent wants to dread going somewhere due to knowing that leaving that place will be horrific for the child and the parent inflicting the disappointment.

JACK

Jack, a 3-year-old boy who is autistic and verbal in some instances and attends a Head Start program daily. He lives with his parents, but his grandmother comes to his house every morning to pick him up and drop him off at school. Jack wakes up at 7:00 AM daily and is ready to go by 7:35 AM. However, Grandma arrives at different times each day; sometimes she gets there at 7:20 and verbally rushes Jack to finish getting ready, and other times she arrives at 8:05 and honks the horn for Jack to run out to the car because they are late. Jack's school starts at 8:15 AM, and if he is late, he has to check in at the front office and can't walk in with his peers. On the days when Grandma is early or late and rushes Jack, he has a meltdown in the car on the way to school that carries over into the first hour of him being in class. The way Jack's day starts often sets the tone for his interactions for the rest of the day. Frustrated by Jack's behaviors when his routine is changed, Grandma has expressed that she will not pick him up anymore until he is "better."

Jack's grandma should

A. Be on time daily or just don't come because Jack will melt down.
B. Work with Jack's parents and teachers to help Jack make transitions no matter what time it is.

You are so smart! How did you know it was B again? Would it help if Grandma was on time daily? Absolutely, but it's not realistic for her. She has a variable schedule and time management issues she needs to work out that are not Jack's problem. If Grandma arrives early at Jack's house, she can sit down and hush, let Jack complete his routine, and then he can leave with her on time. There is no reason to disrupt his process. If Grandma arrives late, she can call Jack's parents and let them know ahead of time how late she will be. Jack can have a "Grandma is late toolkit" that includes specific toys and fidgets that help Jack manage his anxiety. He can also hold a physical picture of Grandma until she gets there. Jack and Grandma can have a car routine of specific songs that they sing on the way to school, and they complete the songs no matter if they are late or not. If Jack has to go into the office, he can sing the office song, and they can create a protocol for how to keep Jack calm and knowledgeable of the next step in this process.

Familiar routines can help Jack when he can't control the timing of things, and it is Grandma's responsibility to enact these for Jack. Lessening the unpredictability helps Jack adjust. Creating a routine for each scenario can help him navigate the changes the way he practiced.

TEST IT OUT

You now have enough info to create some basic accommodations for your kid based on what they need sensory-wise. This will put you on the path to an easier life and a happier kid. Who isn't happy when they are comfortable?

Don't be shy. It is time to put stuff into action.

Don't wait, accommodate!

This process is fairly simple and led by common sense. Use the list of accommodations for ideas in sheet A-2 and write in the ones your kid likes. Use the A-4 to A-4e sheets to organize the helpful information and to see how it will help in each scenario. Accommodations don't have to be fancy, expensive, or perfect. Like if your kid squints all the time, cries when the lights get turned on, and hates looking out the window on car rides, then they probably don't like bright lights. Find a way to accommodate them by dimming the lights for them (use shades, blinds, hats, sunglasses, light dimmers, etc.).

See? Simple.

Remember accommodations just need to be appropriate and helpful.

That's it.

Let your child know what's going on and prep them as much as is needed. Use a visual schedule or verbally answer questions they have about what is coming up next. Then go test out their new accommodations in their everyday spaces.

Chapter 3

THE SKETCH- SET UP FOR SUCCESS

"A meltdown is communication lost in frustration so listen to what they are telling you"

Tools Kits

What you will learn in this section

- What a tool kit is and why you need one
- How to create your own tool kits unique to your child
- How your own self-care is the biggest tool you have and how to use that tool wisely and effectively
- How to test it all out and how practice makes progress on this journey

Anticipate the potential triggers.

Be prepared.

You know your kid, so bring what they need. Have your meltdown tool kit handy.

A tool kit is just what it sounds like. A kit of tools that helps your little one wherever they are. If you want to put the tools in a lunch kit, backpack, or a fanny pack that is easy to carry, the child can hold it themselves most of the time.

You choose what goes in the kit based on what helps your child in the general scenarios they will be in when you are going places. The toolkit for church may need to come stocked with quiet snacks like gummy bears and low-mess art supplies to keep your child engaged and happy.

Expecting them to adapt to an environment in which they need to be quiet and still when they are not naturally quiet nor still will be pointless and unnecessarily frustrating.

It's like forcing a morning person to work at midnight and be happy about it. Or like having a person who is allergic to grass eat all their meals outside picnic style without a blanket. Or having someone who wears glasses go without them all day and expect them to do the same quality of work in the same time frame. Neither of these people would last long in these situations as they go against what they want, need, and who they are. Autistics feel this way all the time. They are expected to "deal with" whatever is socially acceptable in each scenario without modifications that neurotypicals don't require. That's mean and unfair to expect this of your autistic child.

It's also understandable if you have committed this error before. It is not natural for us to see the world from someone else's worldview that is different from our own. We all come with our biases and opinions and tend to not stray unless we are purposefully trying to understand another person. It's uncommonly found naturally but it is not impossible to do.

Let's be honest, how many times did you just want your kid to "behave" without caring to understand what set them off in the first place? We have all been there. Give yourself some grace, then promise to do better and give them what they need to be successful instead of wanting them to be successful without the tools they require for success. Know better, do better.

Have everyone on your child's care team make their own appropriate toolkit based on your child's needs and the environment they will be in. Grandpa's toolkit may have stuff specific to the farm because that's where your child visits him. Auntie's toolkit may have extra snacks, batteries for toys, sunglasses, and hand sanitizer because she likes to hit the road with your little one. Their school toolkit may be much smaller since there should be accommodations in place at school, but a little extra help never hurt.

See the toolbox checklist (sheet A-7) for tips on making your own. Buy some visual schedules that you can use in your school or home tool kits on Etsy.

SELF-CARE

Is this thing on? 🎤 Can ya'll hear me in the back? Good. I want to make sure I'm coming in clear. This message is for you, exhausted and overwhelmed autism parents. Are you listening? Come closer so you can really hear me.

TAKE CARE OF YOURSELF!!!!

Whew. Excuse me for shouting, but it needed to be done this time. Y'all are the absolute worst about taking care of your own needs. We could go into the why behind this phenomenon, but we don't have all day for that therapy session. Just take my word for it and listen to my advice on how to realistically take care of your needs and why it is important to your kid.

Most of the autism parents I have encountered have sensory dysregulation issues, eating and sleeping problems, low fight-or-flight tolerance, and other autistic traits that they learned how to mask a long time ago. Masking is not the same as accommodating.

 Masking pushes things waaaaaay down deep so you don't have to deal with it on the surface of your daily life. Masking is not a fix for the unique presentation of Autism. When you mask your eating issues you could be denying yourself what you want to eat because of societal pressure to eat like an adult so you end up cranky, hungry, and disgusted with the food you have to mask and eat. If you want the chicken nuggets as a 45-year-old and they make you happy, eat the nuggets! You don't have to order off of society's "adult" menu for anyone else's comfort. It goes in your belly and yours alone. Do what you want. Take stock of your own sensory needs and take care of them.

A lot of the things on the accommodations and toolkit list can work for you too. Autistic or not, everyone functions better when their needs are attended to in every environment.

I used to lose my mind when my living room was loud in the afternoons.

Everyone would be talking about different things at once. More than one person was talking to me about different subjects, and I couldn't answer them, multitask, nor hear my own thoughts because everything was piercing my eardrums.

One day, it dawned on me to try some noise-canceling headphones. The first time I put them on was magical. All the sounds dampened immediately. I could hear when someone in front of me was talking to me, but the dreaded background noise was way less intense. To this day, the first time I put on my headphones at the end of each day is a religious experience. My overwhelm starts to melt away, and I am much more apt to be able to take care of things in a state like this. With less overwhelm, I can cook a less rushed dinner, watch an annoying movie with my kids, and do it all without me yelling and crying as much. The headphones, in addition to never letting myself get too hungry, too dehydrated, and too hot, all factor into how my interactions go between me and my family.

I'm not saying all Autistic kids necessarily have Autistic parents. I am saying that more often than not the parents exhibit sensory issues and some social differences at the very least that need to be addressed by the parents.

An example of one of the best reasons to take care of yourself is when your Autistic traits collide with the kid's Autistic traits we have what I like to call a 'Tism Tornado.

For example, my little one is stimming off of Cocomelon at the top volume, while the show playing loudly on repeat has my sensory overload overloading. If I don't take care of my sound sensitivity, then I will lash out at my child, get angry at Cocomelon, and leave my child confused and upset, and me overwhelmed and unable to calm myself.

Our 'tisms have tornadoed, and destruction is left in its wake. Instead, I can be checking my overwhelm levels all the time and do what needs to be done for the well-being of us both.

A second example of the good ole' 'Tism tornado is when we are out and about and I need to stop unplanned and eat something before I feel too hungry. If my kid knows that this is an unplanned stop (and he always knows because he holds the itinerary in the highest regard), then he will protest the stop being necessary, try to get us back on schedule by rushing the stop, all while I am rushing the crew at McDonald's so that I don't pass out before I can get my food. It would be much calmer if my kid would chill while I eat, but his rigidity about the schedule and what could happen if we stray from it takes over his thinking. If I turn around and snap at him to hush and stop rushing me, I was in the wrong because he was just following his instincts. If I had prepped my own snacks, the whole stop could have been avoided.

I find that autism parents are expected to give all of themselves for the good of their children, and that has never felt helpful or realistic to me. It creates parents who are martyrs, who wear the Autism awareness tees everywhere not to actually spread awareness or acceptance, but to alert others to not judge their parenting in public because of their child's autistic outbursts.

Instead, you as a parent can put your child's feelings above public opinion and do whatever you both need to feel comfortable in public, no matter who is watching. Autism parents are so vitally important to the care of their autistic kids, but they are prone to 'tism tornadoes with their own kids in public also.

Know that this next point I am making is only coming from a place of love, so please hear me when I say, that if you don't take care of you, then they can't rely on you to take care of them.

I know you are a parent of an autistic child, so self-care may seem like a luxury, but I assure you, it is not. Paying for every shiny new version of therapy will never help your child as much as a caring, willing, able caregiver will. Find yourself so that you can enter their world with love, not anger and frustration. They feel the vibes you are putting off. It's easier to handle your day when you've slept and eaten well, right? So make it happen for yourself. It's important.

I know how important you are to your kid, so you need to get it together any way you can. Every parent's needs are different. Find what you need and do it.

Other ways for you to take care of yourself include being prepared to tackle the day with your child. For example, make sure you have on running shoes in instances where you know your child will run. Dress for comfort if you don't want to worry about your clothes giving someone a peep show while chasing a toddler. Take your meds, eat well, and get water for yourself.

Don't skip this next step as it is the most important.

Know what you can and cannot handle right now, and don't push past your limits because then they will have to push past theirs too. You think it will be too hot outside to stay non-miserable?

Don't. Go. Outside.

Don't start fights you can't finish or they will finish it for you.

All this boils down to knowing what you need and getting it to make yours and your child's lives easier. Give your child and yourself rewards and praise for managing your accommodations and having whatever you consider to be a successful trip. Ice cream after the zoo. A good nap after the library. A big hug when you get in the car. Make the end rewarding, and it becomes more likely that you both will want to go out again.

Do what you can with your kid based on how you feel. Fed is fed, as long as they have something edible in their bellies. Don't feel bad for "slacking off" today and not doing the absolute most. Just do what you can today to get what you both need.

Use the caregiver energy level A-6 sheet to decide what to engage in based on your energy right now. Doing your best isn't giving your all. It is giving all you can afford to give without bankrupting yourself in other areas.

TEST IT OUT

Now that you have created and tested your accommodations and toolkits, go do it all again! No, really.

Go out as often as you want to. Practice makes progress for you both. Test out new accommodations and tweak old ones. Refine the process as you go.

The more your kid gets out and learns to use their accommodations, advocate for what they need, and learn to lean on your help versus them melting down because they feel unheard and un-helped, the easier going out will be.

A meltdown is communication lost in frustration so listen to what they are telling you.

Chapter 4

THE DRAFT- UNDERSTANDING ABCS AND FUNCTIONS

"When we don't teach kids the correct way to get their needs met and reinforce it, they will do whatever they see or decide is effective"

ABC's

What you will learn in this section

- Advanced behavior assessment and modification tools
- The way Antecedents, Behaviors, and Consequences work together to help your child's behaviors persist
- The Functions of behavior
- How to assess the function your child is communicating to you
- What to do with this new information

ABC's

Woot Woot! You passed part 1 of the book with flying colors. Now, on to the harder stuff.

If your kid is a meltdown mess and all the observations in the world aren't giving you enough insight into what is bothering them, then dig deeper by consulting the ABCs of a situation: the Antecedents, Behaviors, and Consequences. We need to discern the environment the behavior is thriving in to learn how to best handle the communication of a solution.

Antecedents: Think of antecedents as what happens right before the behavior or what the environment is where the behavior happens. Time of day, if they are hungry/tired/congested/dehydrated, presence of certain people, if they are hot/cold, etc.

Behaviors: What you can see that your child is doing. Not what you think they are thinking. We only want the information you can perceive with your five senses. Observable behaviors can include yelling, hitting, screaming, singing, crying, stimming, clinging to you, smiling, running from you, what they are saying, etc.

Consequences: How the behavior is being reacted to by others. Is there reprimand, punishment, getting kicked out, praise, attention, time out, hugs, crying, eye contact, yelling, smiling, clapping, leaving? Put the information into the ABC chart sheet A-1 to visualize how the ABCs fit together and keep behavior going.

When you plug the info you get into the chart, a clear "aha" moment should happen where you figure out why this behavior keeps happening and how to modify either of the three factors to change the behavior or the outcome of the situation.

Use the A-1 Chart to analyze your child's behavior environments and the ways the behavior is encouraged to continue.

After you look at some of your kid's most common behaviors that have stumped you before, return here for more practice with the examples below. Plug these examples into the chart to see how the ABCs go together and what you can do with the resulting information.

HANNAH

Hannah is a semi-verbal 6-year-old who has started biting her 2-year-old brother. She only bites him when she is frustrated from not getting Dad to honor her request right away. She storms off from Dad telling her to wait on her request to be filled, grabs her brother, and bites his arm. Dad comes running, Hannah gets put in time-out, and she sits there nicely for 30 seconds. When she gets out of time-out, she gets the toy she originally requested. Let's check the ABC's:

- A- Hannah wants a toy and her brother is chilling quietly.
- B- Hannah bites her brother after trying unsuccessfully to get Dad to get her the toy.
- C- Hannah goes into a brief time-out out then is given the toy.

If Hannah saw this ritual work once and again to get the toy she wants, she has no reason to stop biting her brother. He is just collateral damage at this point. Biting him is a means to an end for her.

Knowing what we know about Hannah's ABCs, we can use the info to start with the consequences to make change happen.

Instead of a time-out and then the toy being given, have Hannah complete a task for the toy to be given, like cleaning off the table, so that she then understands, "I clean the table, I get the toy." The next time Hannah wants a toy, catch her before she bites her brother, have her perform the task, show you the results, and you immediately go get the toy. This is rerouting Hannah's behavior to doing something positive to get you up and out of your seat instead of something negative like biting.

Her brother will thank you.

When we don't teach kids the correct way to get their needs met and reinforce it, they will do whatever they see or decide is effective. Technically, Hannah was just responding to your ABCs to get what she wants, and now you have to respond to hers to get the appropriate toy-getting behavior out of her.

ADAM

Adam is a fully verbal 12-year-old who has started skipping P.E. class at school and is now getting a phone call home. Adam has always liked sports, so his father is confused as to why Adam is skipping gym. Adam's father talked to him when he got home today, and this is what Adam had to say:

"P.E. is pointless, so I go to the library to study instead. I thought they wouldn't notice that I was gone anyway. They never pick me for teams, and the coach doesn't make them. The kids said I am no good at sports since they know I go to some classes on the Special Education hall, and they don't want me to mess up their games."

Poor Adam. He is hurting and is trying to figure out what to do all alone. Well, Dad is armed with his ABC chart and is going to figure out how to help Adam.

Antecedents: gym class, not getting picked for teams, peers not knowing he is good at sports.

Behaviors: skipping gym class daily, hiding it from parents until school called.

Consequences: will fail gym, but he doesn't care if that happens; possible suspension if he keeps skipping; in trouble at home with parents once they found out; the other kids would still not pick him, but he won't have to be there when they pick others over him.

Adam believes that skipping gym means skipping hurt feelings. Adam did not consider showing his peers his skills to prove that he deserves a chance to play too. Adam did not consider asking the other left-out kids to play with him on their own team. Adam figured that "I don't get picked, so I must not be good; therefore, I deserve to fail, and I'd rather fail for skipping than fail for being embarrassed in front of the mean boys."

Adam's dad gave him some ideas for what to do in gym next time and let him know there would be consequences of losing his PlayStation if he did not find a better solution to gym that didn't involve skipping. Adam's dad also talked to the coach and had them let Adam try out for the track team since he is a good runner and he could show off and feel confident on the field. Adam decided to invite the other kids who don't get picked to play on the other end of the field during gym, and they made up their own games, and they all had a good time together. Adam no longer skips class and is passing gym and Dad praised him for finding a better solution.

The key here was to enforce different consequences and to give Adam ideas for alternate behaviors to handle the antecedents that he had not considered before. Adam solved the issue without forcing himself to do something he was uncomfortable doing (waiting to not get picked for teams and being left out).

WTF: What's the Function?

When confused about the reason behind your kid's behavior just say WTF? or What's The Function of the behavior?

We can determine the function of the behavior or how the behavior is being used to achieve one of 4 things. **A Tangible, sensory input or avoidance, attention, or escape.**

These functions help us to understand other's actions as well as determine why their behaviors are happening. All actions can be sorted into one of the four functions categories of behavior.

Examples of **Tangible** include toys, blankets, snacks, video games or anything that they can hold and use.

Examples of **Sensory Input** or sensory avoidance include hugs, weighted blankets, soft stuffed animals, avoiding high-pitched sounds, avoiding vibrating like a vacuum or dentist drill.

Examples of **Attention** include wanting to play, eye contact, not letting you give others attention, talking to them, watching a show with them, playing games with them, reading to them, and hanging out with them.

Examples of **Escape** include running away, hiding, yelling until they are allowed to leave, kicking over things in their way, and pushing people out of their way.

Solutions for each function include:

Tangible: can they have it or not? If it's appropriate to do so, give it to them. This one is your judgment call. Saying no for control's sake hurts you both so sometimes it is as simple as evaluating your options and saying yes when you can. If they are not allowed to have something, firmly turn them down and offer an alternative. They might still go into a meltdown but giving them the out of "Would you like this instead" gives them options on how to proceed.

Sensory input or Sensory avoidance: some kids like pressure on their faces and will headbutt others or smash their noses into things.

Finding them a safe way to engage in sensory-seeking behaviors is important. Think of what they want and other substitutes that may be more physically safe. Kids who chew on things can have chew necklaces so they won't chew on unsafe things.

The sensory-seeking behavior won't go away, so telling them to stop is frustrating and unhelpful. Sensory avoidance is due autistic people becoming overwhelmed with input from one or more of their senses. They will do whatever they can to avoid the pain sensory discomfort causes. This is not the time to argue with them that no one can hear the light bulbs buzz, so they must be imagining it. Take what they tell you as absolute truth and help them navigate solutions.

Attention: This one is universal to all humans. People like attention for different things, from different people, at different times. Attention affects behavior depending on whether it is given appropriately or not. If I slap you to make you look at me and you turn towards me to yell, it worked. If you slap me and I don't look your way while calmly saying, "We don't slap to get me to look at you, we ask nicely," eventually you will have to ask nicely. Especially if I model asking nicely for you (also move out of the way so you won't get slapped again). The more you feed into giving negative attention, the more they will do the negative behaviors. Give no attention to negative stuff and show them what you want them to do instead. Now, this doesn't mean ignore your kid until they do what you want. It means that people do what they have to, to get what they want, and your kid is no different. Show them a better way to get their needs met, and they will have to use it if there is no other path to getting what they want.

Escape: If I don't want to do something, I will try to get away from the thing. For me, the "thing" is math. I hate it because it is difficult for me. So, even as a child, I would try to be out of class on math days, or I would ask to go to the bathroom during math class to get out of the room for as long as possible. If my teacher understood that my escaping was tied to me feeling incompetent, then she would have offered a tutor and discussed other options for behavior other than running away during class. Autistic children are no different when it comes to escaping. If they can't get you to stop doing the thing they hate, then they will leave. Give them other options.

Be discerning about what they are escaping from, why, and give alternatives. Letting them leave completely does not help them all the time especially if what they are trying to escape from is mandatory. They still have to do the thing, just with extra help or accommodations so find some good ones.

Use the function worksheet A-9 to sort out the reason for your child's behaviors. This is the final piece to the puzzle of behavior. Once we can see what their behaviors are trying to tell us, we can choose how to appropriately respond.

TEST IT OUT

Use the A-1 and A-9 charts to take a closer look at the reasons behind your child's behavior. Do you feel like you understand them any more than you did before you started this book?

I hope so. The next lecture is where we wrap up the investigation and we create a plan for your family to follow.

For the plan to work, the information gathered needs to be solid intel. Meaning try and test out everything you have learned multiple times. Get good at telling what is wrong, why it's going wrong, and how to fix it for your child quickly.

The byproduct of all this practice is that you will be getting closer and closer to your kid since you are entering their world all day, every day now. You will start to see things from their perspective, and it will start to change the way you view the world. The cliché of walking a mile in someone else's shoes is at play here. You have been given the gift of insight into your child's worldview. That is the reason the instructions for getting in your kid's head are concrete, but we never tell you exactly what you will find in there because we don't know.

I've never met your kid so I can't tell you the function of every one of their behaviors but I know that you can. You are with them all the time. We just showed you the most effective way of paying attention and using the information you found.

I'm so proud of you for doing this family introspection work. I know it will pay off for your child to feel more at home in their own family when people start to see what they see. I know you picked up this book for the reason of getting your child to "behave" better but that was not the end goal. The end goal was for them to carve their space in the world with your help.

Autism is a neurological difference that needs no cure. It needs a world full of people who understand and care.

Chapter 5

THE BLUEPRINT-INTERVENTIONS AND THE 2.0 PLAN

"Interventions are the way you insert yourself into the situation to help your child"

CREATE INTERVENTIONS

What you will learn in this section

- How to use the information to map out effective intervention equations
- What a 2.0 plan is and how to create your own
- Information to give other caregivers for your child as a cheat sheet to help them out

Interventions are the way you insert yourself into the situation to help your child. In previous chapters, we focused on what everyone needs and how to get it to them. In this chapter, we focus on the full picture and run through how to troubleshoot issues as they arise. New behaviors will occur but fear not, you have the tools to adapt to autism in any form.

Think of these suggestions as customizable equations to solve the puzzle your child presents to you at any given time, as they are the foundations that can be built upon. Create the equations based on the information you have. If they are hungry, sleepy, and cold, and they are shivering and screaming in their room while you make dinner, then the solution is simple. Oh, it doesn't sound simple? I bet you could figure it out. Test yourself and ask how you would insert yourself into the situation to bring peace to your kid. Now look at the example below. Does it look different from what you would have done? It should look different because every child is different. Make sure yours reflects real information from your child, and you are golden.

Intervention example for a child who is hungry, sleepy, and cold and is shivering and screaming in their room while you make dinner: Provide for their sensory needs first (feed them, get them warm), then do their bedtime routine to soothe them to sleep. The function of the behavior is sensory and tangible. Their goal was not to take your attention away from dinner, so responding to their behavior by teaching proper attention-getting behaviors would not help right now. It would escalate the situation. Now your child is regulated and feeling cared for and heard, and hopefully, they have fallen asleep.

Note: Some schools of parenting will tell you not to give in to your kid's wishes because it is not realistic for how the world works. I wholeheartedly disagree. You can feed into all your kid's needs and teach them how to get their needs met in a "socially acceptable" way. They don't have to mask their autism; they need to learn their unique workaround points to achieve their goals in a neurotypical coded world.

Parenting shouldn't be about raising obedient children. It should be about helping your child find and share their voice by thinking critically and being introspective.

EVALUATE INTERVENTIONS

Did it work?

Did the interventions you tried help your child soothe themselves?

If not, try again with a different intervention. Evaluate the issue. Did you pick the correct function of their behavior? Is the environment one in which the destructive behaviors are encouraged to continue?

Prime example of "try, try again" in a real-world example below.

The dreaded after-school-before-bed witching hour 💀 🪄.

It's 7:30 pm, and you go to help your older child with their homework. Your little autistic muffin throws all of her toys on the floor and breaks them as soon as you leave her room. You question what you are doing to encourage this behavior.

Is your little one wanting your attention since you are giving it to their brother? Probably not, because they wait to destroy things after you leave instead of in your face. Are they trying to escape playing alone? Nope, because they stay in their room and don't go looking for a playmate. Are they asking for something tangible? Nope, that's not it either, as they have not requested anything. Are they looking for sensory input from crunching and breaking? Yep, this is the function that is motivating their behavior. It does not require your attention. In fact, it thrives in your inattention, and your child knows how to get their need for sensory input when you leave them alone. There is nothing more satisfying than breaking all the arms off their Barbies, as those pops are the right kind of satisfying.

You incorrectly assume they want attention since you are giving it to their brother, so you take them into the brother's room with you both, and they kick and scream, and you get frustrated. If the function of their behavior was attention, giving them attention would have stopped the behavior, right? Since they were clawing at you to get back to their room, you decided that the function was sensory after all. Once you realize their sensory need, you give them a bucket with dry macaroni for them to crush with a rubber mallet in the room with you and brother, and they are thrilled with this new sound.

After your son's homework is finished, you transition to folding laundry and clean up the decapitated Barbies in your daughter's room. Your little one screams as you put the Barbies away because they were not finished popping them. You give up and leave the Barbies out, leaving their room a mess, and go fold laundry. You know how to pick your battles, and battling Barbies is not on today's to-do list. You return to their room when you hear screams as they have emptied the macaroni bucket and are stepping on the hard pieces that are hurting their feet now.

At this point, you are done for the night. You are hungry and tired, and you realize you skipped your afternoon snack. No wonder you are so over everything. You grab a granola bar and a Snickers, chase them with a bottle of water, and get ready for round two with your daughter.

You check their ABCs: them being alone and sensory seeking is the antecedent, the behavior is seeking cracking sounds and tactile input, and the consequence is the look of exasperation on your face. They never have to clean up their mess or move to the next thing in a healthy way, as they are just being shuffled around the house. You change their ABCs by having them by your side, doing the popping and crunching activity with them, and having them clean up their area as they go when they get bored with that sensory bin. You go on the hunt for another sensory input item together.

Laundry can wait. It wouldn't get done right now anyway, as your child needs your focus. After they play themselves into hunger and finish the sensory play, you make them a quick dinner they can feed themselves at their own pace and let them watch YouTube videos on the TV while you sit in the adjoining room and fold the laundry with minimal interruption. You grab some dinner for yourself and let your oldest know to come eat too. They sit with their sibling while you eat and take your afternoon meds to help you sleep well through the night.

There is peace and quiet for a minute other than the sound of YouTube, so you get 20 minutes to doom-scroll TikTok while your little one finishes eating. Then you get them ready for bed. The nighttime routine was not half as draining tonight because they were calm and worn out from sensory play. They are full and content, which gives them a calmer and regulated disposition.

They get into bed willingly and let you fall asleep with them. You stay in the bed with them for three hours until you wake up with your left arm asleep from laying in an awkward position. You get up, go watch an adult show, and have uninterrupted ice cream while your kids sleep. Eventually, you prep for tomorrow, then lay down and wait for the day to start all over again. Everyone has what they need, including you, so this afternoon didn't turn out that bad.

I illustrate how our lives with our autistic babies look different from neurotypical families, but all families have difficulties. Our kids become teenagers, and we don't worry as much about drugs and sex, but we do worry about peer pressure and safety. Our kids go to middle school, and we worry about them not having friends instead of neurotypical families worrying about their kid not making the soccer team. We all have something to worry about. There is **no gold medal in the struggle Olympics**, and there is no reason to prove to others how tough you have it. They wouldn't understand anyway, as all of us struggle differently. Celebrate your wins and vent about your low days with people who get it. Autism parent support groups can be great places for these interactions.

It helps with autism awareness and acceptance for us to tackle the misconceptions of what we have to "deal with" in taking care of our kids so that people will know how they can actually help us. Tackle this with people who are not committed to misunderstanding you. Sharing the new interventions with your dad, who is going to tell you your child just "needs the belt to straighten him out," is not going to help anyone. Some people have no intention of understanding your beautiful baby. That's a them problem. The last thing you want to hear is, "I don't know how you do it," when they don't even know what "it" is. They just equate autism with a difficult life, so they never see the amazing child your little muffin is. That's sad for them.

We, as special needs parents, have gotten so used to being strong parents that we forgot how to just be parents. All parents love **and** get tired of their kids. Two things can be true at once, but the same way no kid is better than another, no parent is better than another either. Let's focus on how to help ourselves instead of wasting energy comparing our struggles. This isn't an "all kids matter so we shouldn't complain" plea; instead, it is a "focus on your own stuff and how to make your life better rather than worrying about Karen's pity for you that is unwarranted, misinformed, and misplaced."

Hopes and the 2.0 plan

Tell me your hopes for the way your family will run.

What do you want to get out of this book? I could have asked you this at the beginning but I wanted you to feel hope first of what is possible for you instead of the defeat you have been feeling from what has been happening before you learned this new info...

Tell me how you want bath time to go. How breakfast time could look. Or how the ride to school can be filled with songs and giggles. I want you to be ridiculously and delusionally hopeful about how the scenarios in your house can improve. Write this down in your hopeful Family 2.0 plan, area by area, issue by issue. Get specific and take your time with your wishes, as what you put into the plan is what you get out of it. Get specific and exact.

For example, you want more downtime without screams during the day, but instead of that, you write, "I want to wake up at 4 a.m. to get 1 hour of peace alone," but you know you are not a morning person. You say, "That is what the mom blogger does, and it works for her!" Then you realize your mistake. You, fortunately, are not her. The goal doesn't fit you personally. Instead, write what you want ("at least 2 hours of quiet-ish time per day"), and then we will figure out the best way for your particular family to get it.

We will take your Hopeful Family 2.0 plan (sheet A-5) and the information on how your family works currently and start to bridge the gap. The result is a plan that actually works instead of a plan that you will never get used to because it works against the way your family communicates, sleeps, eats, or gathers. Work with your family's uniqueness, not against it.

Complete the hopeful family plan before continuing to the next step.

The Hopeful 2.0 plan and your Final 2.0 plan will have the same sections and headings. There are 9 sections on the template but you don't have to use each one. Below are some suggestions for sections on your plan. You can use places you frequent that your child does not do well in, times of day that are currently stressful, or events that happen that you want to prepare for.

- Morning routine
- Evening routine
- Bedtime
- Weekend mornings
- Homework time
- Church

- Aunt Bri's house
- Grocery shopping
- Na na's job
- Going to the rodeo
- What to do at the zoo
- Movie theater routine
- In the car rider line after school waiting for brother
- Ride to school in the morning
- Leaving the park
- The pet store
- Baseball practice
- Accepting No from Dad
- Respecting boundaries with Mom

The sections on everyone's sheet will be different and personal to their family. Below is an example to give you an idea of how the Hopeful plan will look.

1. Weekend mornings

- Kids are up anytime after 8 am and they get their own breakfast.
- They don't bother parents until after 10 am.
- They have fully charged tablets and TV remotes to use independently.
- No one is fighting and they stay relatively quiet until lunchtime.

- Parents leave their room after 10 if desired and can have a quiet breakfast together.
- Hot or cold breakfast options are available and accessible to all.

2. In the car rider line after school waiting for brother
- Sing songs together or discuss kids' day
- Dad reads to the kid or watch a video together
- Kid plays in the backseat
- Kid's seat belt on when driving off without fuss
- Everyone is cool and comfortable during the wait

3. The pet store
- Leave at the end with no tears and no fuss
- Buy at least one toy at or under budget
- Stay no more than 30 minutes- no asking for more time
- Can ask staff 3 questions at the most

4. Accepting no from Dad
- Nodding "yes" that the
- No is understood No stomping feet or rolling on the floor
- Accept one of the three alternatives given
- No yelling or repeating self from Dad

If you read the plan and rolled your eyes, then it did its job! It is supposed to feel like it's a fantasy so that you have something to reach for. Even if it does not end up perfectly you still would have made vast improvements. That peace you felt while writing out what you fantasize about having is attainable.

To find this peace grab your Hopeful list and the other information you have gathered in the previous lessons and write out how things are going currently so we know where we are starting. We will call this your Right now sheet. You can write this info on a clean copy of the A-5 sheet. It will end up looking like the example below.

1. Weekend mornings
   - Kids up at 5 am in parent's bed begging for breakfast.
   - The tablets are dead from the day before and can't find the remotes so parents are disturbed again
   - Kids fight loudly until parents get up to stop them, with the kids' intention of fighting being to get the parents out of bed.
   - Parents start the day with no alone time
   - All food has to be prepared by parents so kids have no access.

2. In the car rider line after school waiting for brother

   - Kid crying in the car if the line is long
   - Dad plays on the phone until annoyed by the kid crying then Dad yells for quiet
   - Kid hops from the back to the front of car

- Kid cries and kicks when it is time to put the seat belt back on
- Everyone hot and miserable in the line daily

3. The pet store

- Leaves at the end having to be drug out by mom
- Screams until mom buys all the things they want that are over budget
- Stays for an hour each time due to crying for more time every time it is time to leave
- Follows staff around asking them multiple questions even after mom tries to redirect them

4. Accepting no from Dad

- Yelling "I hate you" when told no
- Stomping feet or rolling on the floor
- Refuses all alternatives while threatening to yell if request is not filled
- Dad yells, sends kid away, or gets physical when kid acts out of anger

Does this second list sound more like how life is right now? I thought so. Let's transform the Right Now list into the Final Plan by filling it with solutions from the A-4 to A-4e, A-7 sheet, and the interventions you came up with. I know it looks hard at first, but I believe in you. You now have the tools to let your creativity fly and equip you to make the Final Plan work.

Write the Final plan on blank sheets of paper or type it since it is going to be lengthy and written in sentence form so that you can make sense of the actions you need to take and a bullet list isn't explicit enough. Check out an example of a section of the Final plan below.

1. Weekend mornings

- Kids each have a labeled basket with their preferred cold breakfast options, their charged preferred device, and a picture of the rewards they get if they don't go into their parent's room until instructed. Tablets have alarms on them to go off at 10 am so kids know when parents are to be awake. When parents emerge and kids have fought or disturbed parents the appropriate amount of reward pictures will be taken away and whatever pictures are left will be exchanged for the rewards. If parents go out of the room to break up fighting, they do so and then return to their room. They do not add the consequence of them waking up and doing things for the behavior of kids fighting. After 10 am parents fix breakfast and return to the room to eat together if they wish and kids eat the hot breakfast made by the parents in their own space with their devices. Family time starts after breakfast is cleared away then devices can stay or go based on plans for the day. Schedule for the day is presented now to the kids and the day begins for everyone together.

That was easy, huh? I told you it would be. It all sounds good on paper, but we don't know where to tweak the plan until you test it out. Let's say you tried out the plan for the last four Saturdays and found that leaving the devices out didn't work because the kids would go get them the night before after you went to sleep, then stay up all night playing when they weren't supposed to. Knowing this info helps you recognize that you need to put a password on the device and leave it out. Let them come into your room once they get up, and you unlock it then and leave it unlocked until they are finished with the device for the day. You can also turn off the WiFi at night and only turn it back on in the morning at the agreed-upon time.

The plan is supposed to change as your kid changes, your regular schedule changes, and your family's needs change. Make it a habit to check on your plan (after it is tested and proven to work) at least every 3 months to determine if anything needs to be adjusted.

Making the plan is a big ole labor of love in the beginning since it will take time and reflection to make but boy is it worth it to see on paper how you will transform the culture and vibe in your home.

TEST IT OUT

The final test is continuing to use the skills you learned in this book and the Final plan to guide your family through the tough times. There will be tough times but honey you are tougher!

Whenever a new behavior occurs that you have never experienced with your child, return to the book and determine what the behavior is communicating to you and how you need to respond in order to help your kid and yourself.

You. Got. This.

If you read this book and the plan feels too big to make on your own, there are individual coaching plans available that I offer where I assess all of the behaviors and make the full plan for you.

Chapter 6

YOU'RE DONE!

"The final test is continuing to use the skills you learned in this book and the final plan to guide your family through the tough times. There will be tough times but honey you are tougher!"

Congrats! You Finished

You made it to the end of this book, and you are now a behavior pro and Zen family master. Congrats! Open the certificate, put your name and date on it, and enjoy the fruits of your labor.

This certificate is purely for your wall or refrigerator, as it indicates nothing other than that you invested in yourself and your family's well-being. This does not certify you as any professional anything, so just admire your hard work, okay?

Make sure you are subscribed to the M Perfect crew so that you can be informed about all the behavior-related books we have coming up next!

All the best,

Meghan Ashley, LPC-S

WORKSHEETS

ABC CHART

Antecedents	Behaviors	Consequences

ACCOMMODATION IDEAS

Pull ideas from our list then come up with your own accommodations lists below sorted by senses.

- Coffee grounds for cleansing smells
- Sunglasses
- Neck pillow
- Ice pack
- Noise cancelling headphones
- Loop ear plugs

- Oil roll-on for scent
- Face mask to block smells
- Tablet/protable gaming
- Wrist flashlight
- Favorite non-perishable snacks
- Weighted blanket/vest/stuffed animal

- Jacket with hood
- Hat
- Eye mask
- Favorite drink/water bottle
- Wrist leash/backpack leash
- Hand sanitizer/wipes
- Personal fan
- Portable heating pad

SIGHT

SOUND

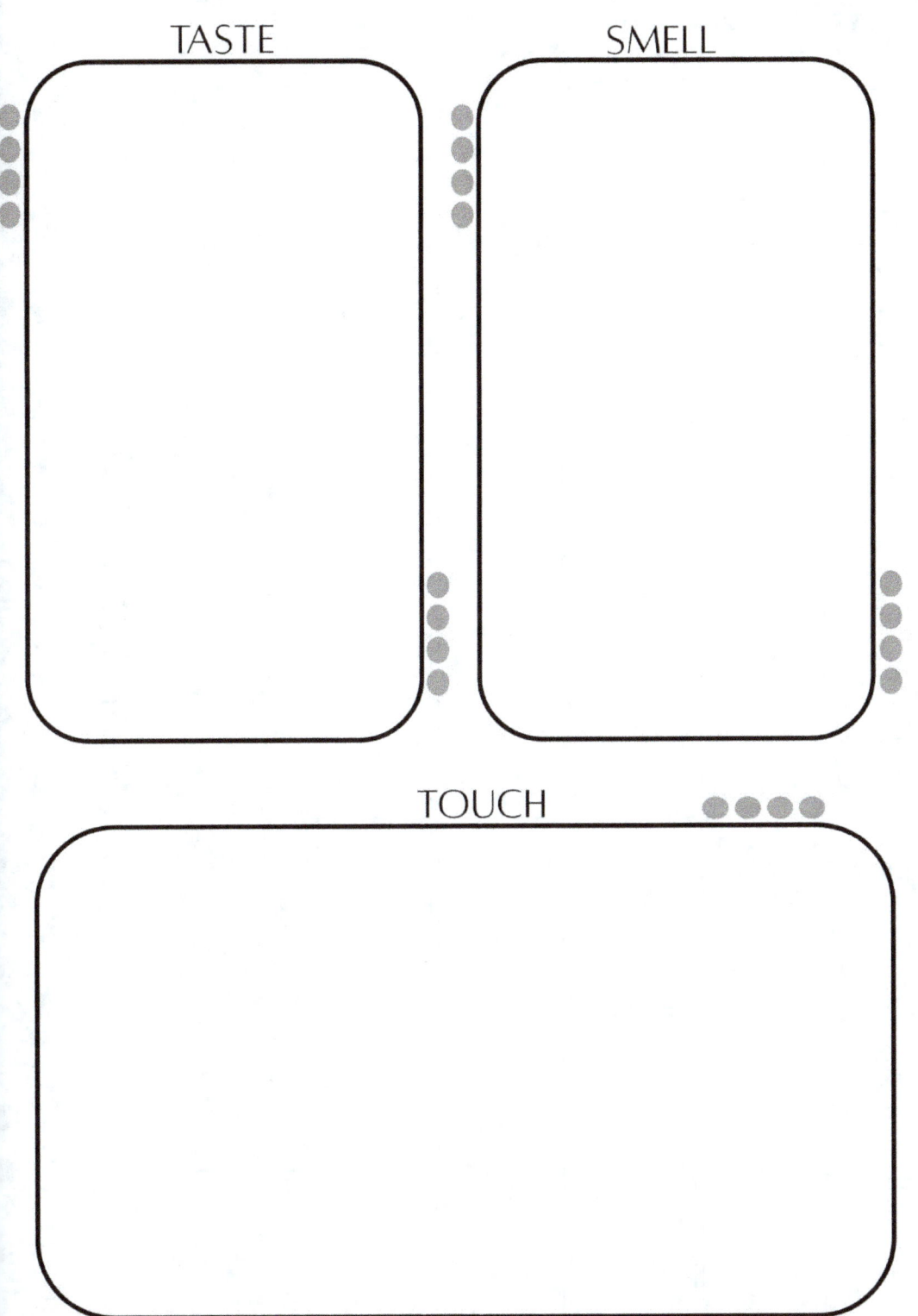

TASTE

SMELL

TOUCH

Scenario(difficulties)

Senses					
Sight					
Sound					
Smell					
Taste					
Touch					

Scenario(Accommodations)

Senses	Sight	Sound	Smell	Taste	Touch

Scenario(Resolutions)

Senses						
Sight						
Sound						
Smell						
Taste						
Touch						

Scenario(Example)

Below is an example of how to fill out the charts. Not every scenario has a difficulty that needs to be addressed. Some blocks will be blank. In the example, all of the three charts are combined in one. In reality, there are more difficulties and accommodations per block which is why more space is given above by separating the charts.

Senses	CHURCH	CAR AFTER SCHOOL	CAR BEFORE SCHOOL	GRANNY'S HOUSE	BROTHER'S KARATE	MOVIE THEATER	GIRL SCOUTS
Sight	DIF: LIGHTS TOO BRIGHT IN AM ACM: SIT TO THE RIGHT WERE THE SUN IS LESS VISIBLE RES: LESS WIGGLING DUE TO LIGHT IN EYES	DIF: EYES TIRED FROM THE DAY ACM: NECK PILLOW TO REST HEAD AND EYE COVER RES: ABLE TO SPEAK ABOUT DAY WITHOUT LOOKING AT MOM PAINFULLY	DIF: SUN UP AND IN EYES ACM: SHADES ON THE WINDOWS RES: ARRIVE AT SCHOOL NOT AGITATED SINCE EYES HURT		DIF: TOO MUCH MOVEMENT TO LOOK AT ACM: TABLET IN THE CORNER FACING THE WALL RES: QUIET AND HAPPY ALONE NOT HELP OR WHINING ALONE WITHOUT CONTACT FORCED TO WATCH	DIF: CANT SEE SNACKS ACM: ON WRIST DIM SMALL FLASHLIGHT RES: ABLE TO EAT IN AND NOT REQUIRE EYE CONTACT	DIF: EYE CONTACT EXPECTED ACM: PRIVATE CONVO WITH LEADERS TO JUM RES: FEELING LIKE HARMFUL EYE CONTACT IS NOT NECESSARY
Sound	DIF: LOUD MUSIC UNEXPECTEDLY ACM: NOISE CANCELLING HEADPHONES RES: ABLE TO SIT IN SANCTUARY WITH DAD	DIF: BROTHER TALKING TOO LOUD ACM: LOOP EAR PLUGS TO REDUCE SHARP SOUNDS RES: ABLE TO INTERACT WITH BROTHER		DIF: TV PLAYS LOUD ALL THE TIME ACM: LOOP EAR PLUGS AND PLAY IN ROOM FURTHEST AWAY FROM THE LIVING ROOM RES: LESS IRRITATION	DIF: LOUD KARATE SOUNDS ACM: NOISE CANCELLING HEADPHONES THAT PLUG INTO TABLET RES: CAN ONLY HEAR TABLET NOISE THAT IS WANTED	DIF: MOVIE TOO LOUD ACM: LOOP EAR PLUGS ASK TO SIT AS FAR AWAY FROM THE SPEAKERS AS POSSIBLE RES: MORE COMFORTABLE VOLUMES	DIF: TOO MANY VOICES TO CONCENTRATE ON ACM: SIT NEAR MAIN SPEAKER, WEAR LOOPS IN FLESH TONE WHEN INTERACTING RES: LESS BACKGROUND NOISE

	Scenario 1	Scenario 2	Scenario 3	Scenario 4	Scenario 5	Scenario 6
Smell				DIF: SMELLS LIKE MOTHBALLS / ACM: ROLL ON OF PEPPERMINT IN POCKET / RES: CAN SMELL WHAT THEY WANT	DIF: SMELLS LIKE FEET / ACM: MASK WITH PEPPERMINT OIL IN IT / RES: CAN SMELL WHAT THEY WANT AND IT IS CONSTANT	DIF: POPCORN SMELL IS NAUSEATING / ACM: SHAKER WITH TOP FILLED WITH COFFEE BEANS / RES: PALATE CLEANSER SO SMELL DOES NOT LINGER
						DIF: HATES POPCORN / ACM: OTHER SNACKS OFFERED / RES: A FED KID
Taste	DIF: FOOD IN CAFETERIA IS GROSS / ACM: OWN SNACKS ARE BROUGHT AND STAFF IS INFORMED OF FOOD AVERSIONS / RES: NOT HUNGRY AND ANGRY	DIF: HUNGRY AFTER SCHOOL / ACM: COMFORTING SNACKS IN A BAG IN THE CAR / RES: NOT HUNGRY AND ANGRY	DIF: EATS BREAKFAST TOO SLOW TO EAT AT HOME / ACM: CHOOSE BETWEEN 3 "POPPABLE" BREAKFASTS THAT ARE PORTIONED BY HOW LONG THEY TAKE TO EAT / RES: EATS WITHOUT BEING RUSHED SINCE THEY HAVE THE RIGHT AMOUNT	DIF: GRANNY DOESNT COOK WHAT THEY LIKE / ACM: ENCOURAGE THEM TO TRY GRANNY'S FOODS BUT HAVE LUNCH BOX FULL OF PREFERRED FOODS READY AS WELL. / RES: NOT FEELING PRESSURED TO MASK AND HAS COMFORT FOODS AVAILABLE	DIF: GRANNY AND POP POP WANTS KID TO SIT ON COUCH ALL THE TIME / ACM: MAKE A COMFY SPOT IN LIVING ROOM FOR KID BASED OFF THEIR TACTILE SPECIFICATIONS / RES: THEY CAN BE SUPERVISED BUT DON'T HAVE TO BE ON THE SCRATCHY COUCH OR BE TOUCHED BY GRANDPARENTS	
Touch	DIF: ALL THE OLDER WOMEN WANT TO HUG / ACM: PARENT HOLD'S HAND OR PICKS UP KID SO OTHER'S CAN'T TOUCH. / RES: KID ONLY HAS DESIRED TOUCH FROM PARENT AND NONE FROM STRANGERS	DIF: SEATBELTS ARE HOT / ACM: PUT BLANKETS OVER SEATBELTS WHEN KID GETS OUT IN THE MORNING / RES: ROOM TEMP SEATBELTS AVOID BURNING HOT BELTS	DIF: HATES THE RESTRICTING FEEL OF THE SEATBELT ON CHEST / ACM: LET THEM COUNT TO HOWEVER LONG IT TAKES TO GET TO SCHOOL SO THEY CAN KNOW HOW MANY SECONDS IT IS UNTIL THEY CAN UNBUCKLE / RES: IT IS NO LONGER AN UNKNOWN HOW LONG THE DISCOMFORT IS			

2.0 PLAN

A-5

Caregiver Energy Tasks

_____
_____
_____
_____
_____
_____
_____
_____
_____
_____
_____
_____
_____

Low Energy Tasks

Fill in the list to the left with things you can do
when your tank is empty but still have to show
up as a caregiver.
Ex: sit on the floor with the kids while they play
Play I spy with the kids
Frozen pizza or takeout for dinner
Play music and have a sing along together
Press play and let a youtuber read to the kids
Close you and the kids in the same room and le
them do whatever they want and clean up late

Medium Energy Tasks

Fill in the list to the right with things you
can do when you have a little (but not a
bunch) to give as a caregiver.
Ex: Play hide and seek or Marco Polo
Make healthy under 30 minute meal
Let the kids help with cooking
Go for a walk around the block with the
kids
Read a book to the kids with animated
voices

_____
_____
_____
_____
_____
_____
_____
_____
_____
_____
_____
_____
_____
_____

_____
_____
_____
_____
_____
_____
_____
_____
_____
_____
_____
_____
_____

High Energy Tasks

Fill in the list to the left with things you can do
when your cup is overflowing and you are feeling
full of energy to be a caregiver.
Ex: Run around and play tag with the kids
Cook a full meal with leftovers for later
Do Yoga/Zumba/Cardio/Go for a run
Act out a movie scene with the kids
Do arts and crafts
Have a yes day and do whatever the kids sugges

MY TOOLBOX CHECKLIST

GHT:

- ○ ....
- ○ ....
- ○ ....
- ○ ....

MELL:

- ○ ....
- ○ ....
- ○ ....
- ○ ....

OUND:

- ○ ....
- ○ ....
- ○ ....
- ○ ....

STE:

- ○ ....
- ○ ....
- ○ ....
- ○ ....

OUCH:

- ○ ....
- ○ ....
- ○ ....
- ○ ....

MY TOOLKIT IDEAS

TOUCH

- GLOVES
- FIDGET TOYS
- STRESS BALLS
- SENSORY BINS
- BITING NECKLACE
- WEIGHTED BLANKET
- STUFFED ANIMAL
- FAVORITE TOY
- FAVORITE BLANKET/ PILLOW
- COMFORTABLE CLOTHING
- NO TAG CLOTHING
- FIDGET JEWELRY
- STRAWS
- PIPE CLEANERS
- THERAPY PUTTY
- HAND SANITIZER

TASTE

- SNACKS
- MINTS
- TIC TACS
- GUM
- DRINKS
- WATER
- FAVORITE FOODS
- LOLLIPOPS
- HONEY STICKS

SMELL

- FACE MASK
- DEODORIZER SPRAY
- NOSE PLUGS
- THINGS THAT SMELL
- LIKE HOME
- CLOTHING THAT SMELLS
- LIKE CAREGIVER
- SOOTHING OILS

SOUND

- RECORDING OF FAVORITE
- PHRASES
- TAPE RECORDER
- FAVORITE SONGS
- TOY THAT MAKES SOUNDS
- TABLET/ GAMING DEVICE
- NOISE CANCELLING
- HEADPHONES
- NOISE CANCELLING EAR
- PLUGS

SIGHT

- SENSORY LIGHT TOY
- SUNGLASSES
- PICTURES OF HOME OR OF FAVORITE
- PLACES OR PEOPLE
- KEYCHAIN OR JEWELRY OF FAVORITE
- ANIMAL
- ART SUPPLIES TO DRAW
- NOTEBOOK TO WRITE
- INFO ON CURRENT FIXATION (WEBISTE,
- VIDEO, OR BOOK)

WTF KID?

Find the function of each behavior (Tangible, Escape, Sensory Input, Attention) your child has and put it in the table below. Go to the behavior, find the function, then do the first intervention. If that doesn't help, try the second one or other interventions that work on that function.

Behavior	Function	Try first	Try second
Example Stand in front of the tv	Attention	Talk to him about the show	Act out the scene in the show with him

CERTIFICATE
OF MPERFECTION

THIS IS TO CERTIFY THAT

Has successfully completed the
Blueprint to Behavior Book

Meghan Ashley

Instructor

Date

www.ingramcontent.com/pod-product-compliance
Lightning Source LLC
Chambersburg PA
CBHW060339130626
46553CB00003B/1054